BE THE CHANGE!

ANIMAL RIGHTS

BLOOD MONEY ACRES

END SPECIES ISM!

UNITE FOR ANIMAL JUSTICE

HOW YOU CAN MAKE A DIFFERENCE

Cynthia O'Brien

BROWN BEAR BOOKS

Published by Brown Bear Books Ltd

4877 N. Circulo Bujia
Tucson, AZ 85718
USA

and

G14, Regent Studios
1 Thane Villas
London N7 7PH
UK

© 2024 Brown Bear Books Ltd

ISBN 978-1-78121-943-0 (ALB)
ISBN 978-1-78121-949-2 (paperback)

Library of Congress Cataloging-in-Publication Data available on request

Design Manager: Keith Davis
Children's Publisher: Anne O'Daly
Picture Manager: Sophie Mortimer

Picture Credits
Cover: iStock: Doro Carls Yague (background); Shutterstock: Atlas Studio. Interior: Alamy: Associated Press 19, WENN Rights Ltd 23; iStock: SDI Productions 26; Shutterstock: Gerard Bottino 27, bruna-nature 8, Vickey Chauhan 7b, Ringo Chiu 5, Dragon Images 25, Flash Studio 16, Craig Fraser10, Jessica Girvan 18, Gorodenkoff 22, Dan Holm 24, Ben Houdijk 21, Ian Davidson Photography 13, Marcio Isensee 9, I am James Anthony 4, Oleg Kharkhan 7t, Melissamn 14, New Africa 15, podyom 12, Prostock-studio 17, Fomin Serhii 11; Time For Kids: Beth Redwood/Marvel Hero Project

All artwork and other photography Brown Bear Books.

Brown Bear Books has made every attempt to contact the copyright holder.
If you have any information about omissions, please contact: licensing@brownbearbooks.co.uk

Manufactured in the United States of America
CPSIA compliance information: Batch#AG/5657

Websites
The website addresses in this book were valid at the time of going to press. However, it is possible that contents or addresses may change following publication of this book. No responsibility for any such changes can be accepted by the author or the publisher. Readers should be supervised when they access the Internet.

Contents

What Are Animal Rights?

All people are entitled to basic human rights. These include the right to food and to live free from slavery. The animal rights movement argues that animals should have similar rights, such as the right to live freely and be safe from harm.

People deny animal rights by using them for food and clothing, for science experiments, factory farming, and more. People keep animals in captivity on farms or as entertainment in zoos and marine parks. Animal rights activists fight against all these practices. They eat a vegan or vegetarian diet and refuse to wear leather. Animal welfare activists argue for the ethical treatment of animals. However, these protestors may not be opposed to eating meat or using animal products.

The Five Freedoms

In 1965, a report in the United Kingdom outlined some rules for animal welfare. Fourteen years later, these became the Five Freedoms: freedom from hunger or thirst; freedom from discomfort; freedom from pain, injury, or disease; freedom to express normal behavior; and freedom from fear and distress.

Sanctuaries provide safe spaces for animals. The Phuket Elephant sanctuary in Thailand rescues elephants that have worked in tourism or the logging industry.

Campaigners held regular actions outside the Farmer John slaughterhouse in Vernon, California, from 2017. They were protesting about the way animals were treated there. The place was shut down in February 2023.

Fighting for Rights

The Five Freedoms have become recognized around the world and part of some welfare laws. But animal rights activists argue that these rules do not go far enough, especially when animals are raised for food.

The Royal Society for the Prevention of Cruelty to Animals Organizations in the United Kingdom is the oldest animal rights group in the world. It was founded in 1824. Many other animal rights and protection groups have followed, including People for the Ethical Treatment of Animals (PETA) and Cruelty Free International.

Organizations such as The World Organization for Animal Health and World Animal Protection focus on animal welfare issues. International Fund for Animal Welfare and the Humane Society also focus on protecting animals.

Chapter 1

Understanding the Arguments

Speciesism is the idea that the human species, is superior to, or better than, other animal species. This belief has led people to use and control animals for their own needs or wants. It has also led to cruelty and mistreatment.

Not all people believe that humans are more important than animals. For thousands of years, Indigenous communities around the world lived in harmony with nature. For example, the Plains people in the United States honored and respected the buffalo. They depended on it for food, clothing, tools, and shelter, but they only killed the animals they needed. Everything changed when European settlers arrived.

Emergency Files

Overhunting

European settlers killed millions of buffalo across the American plains. Mainly, they killed them for sport and to make way for new railroads, towns, and farms. By the end of the 1800s, there were only 300 buffalo left in the wild. Since then, people have overhunted other land animals around the world and overfished the oceans for sea creatures such as cod and whales. This led to dangerously decreased animal populations and damaged ecosystems.

Chickens called "broilers" are raised for meat. Tens of thousands are crammed into a shed.

Today's Issues

The demand for meat has never been higher. Factory farming has become one way to satisfy this demand. People also kill animals for their skins to make leather goods. Ducks and geese are used for meat and stripped of their feathers to fill pillows and coats. Zoo and other show animals live away from their natural habitats, sometimes in poor conditions. Animals are used to test cosmetics and medicines. People also hunt and kill animals for sport. Animal trafficking is a big, but illegal business. People capture wild animals for sale as pets, to use their skin for clothing, and other body parts for decoration and medicines.

The pangolin is the most trafficked animal. People use the claws and scales in medicines and fashion, and its meat is a delicacy in some countries.

Elephants have been seen helping calves that are not related to them, helping them in and out of rivers, for example.

The Science

Centuries ago, people were aware of animals as sentient beings, but they did little to protect them. Even today, few national laws protect all animals and many countries do not recognize animal sentience in their laws. Recognizing all animal sentience is a key part of the animal rights movement.

Animals Have Feelings

Scientists know that many species have emotions such as sadness, joy, anger, or fear. Studies have focused on mammals such as apes and elephants. In the 1960s, Jane Goodall began studying chimpanzees in Tanzania, Africa. Her findings showed that chimpanzees were intelligent creatures with emotions.

Scientists studying elephants discovered they have empathy. This means that they can understand another elephant's feelings. For example, elephants try and cheer each other up when they are sad. Other animals show a range of emotions. Dolphins are happy when they recognize their friends. Some people think that only mammals are sentient, but studies have shown that fish feel pain and that insects can be fearful.

About 77% of the world's usable land is used for raising cattle or growing crops for animal feed.

Climate Change

Greenhouse gases are the main drivers of climate change. Animal agriculture contributes about 18 percent of these gases, including methane and nitrous oxide. Forests help to absorb the gases, but people cut them down to make way for grazing lands and to grow food for cattle. The meat industry also uses a lot of water, which is a precious resource for Earth's future.

Climate change badly affects wild animals. It threatens food and water sources and causes droughts, floods, and wildfires that destroy habitats. Healthy animal and plant life is crucial to a healthy planet. Working for animal rights is also helping to protect Earth.

Chapter 2

Political Action

Laws concerning animals are complicated. They can leave animals unprotected or captive. In many cases, laws need to be much stronger and better enforced. New laws are also needed. Political action is one way to make this happen.

The Animal Legal Defense Fund is working to stop people from capturing and selling animals such as giraffes and elephants

Two books sparked a wide interest in animal rights and the need for better laws. In 1964, Ruth Harrison published *Animal Machines*. The book raised awareness of factory farming and animal suffering. Peter Singer's book, *Animal Liberation*, published in 1975, argues that all animals, human and non-human, are equal. Singer's book launched the modern animal rights movement.

Animals and the Law

The Animal Legal Defense Fund, based in the United States, uses the legal system to protect animals. Lawyers, law students, and other workers are helping to make laws that help and advance animal rights. They have had many successes. Their work has stopped bear hunting in California and helped ban the sale of cosmetics tested on animals in ten states.

It is not easy to release captive animals that are used to living in a zoo. Releasing them in groups may help them readjust to the wild.

Non-Human Clients

There is a growing group of lawyers who specialize in animal law for non-human clients. The Non-Human Rights Project (NhRP) is a group, based in the United States, that is fighting for the rights of elephants, apes, and dolphins. Their clients include Happy, an elephant held at the Bronx Zoo. NhRP is hoping to win Happy's freedom, just as lawyers in Argentina won freedom for Cecilia, a chimpanzee. A judge in that case ruled that Cecilia had the rights of a legal person. She was freed from a city zoo and taken to a sanctuary.

A Global Fight

There is no international law that protects all animals. Laws between countries and even within countries can differ widely. Some countries have no protection laws at all. Animal rights activists hope to change this. The Convention on Animal Protection (CAP) is one such treaty while Global Animal Law (GAL) has prepared a UN Convention on Animal Health and Protection along with the United Nations. If an international convention is adopted, it would be a big step forward for animal rights around the world.

Cruelty Free International

Since 1898, Cruelty Free International has been battling to end all experiments on animals. Animals are used by scientists to test medicines, cosmetics, and other products. CFI has forced many companies to stop animal testing and experiments. Companies that have stopped this testing earn CFI's seal of approval, the "Leaping Bunny" logo.

Rescuers evacuate dogs from Ukraine, following the Russian invasion. A number of charities specialize in rescuing animals from war and disaster zones.

Speak Up

PETA Campaigns

Since it began in 1988, PETA has become a powerful animal rights group around the world. PETA campaigns against using animals for food, in fashion, in laboratories, and for entertainment. The group sometimes uses shocking images in advertisements, such as fur covered in fake blood. PETA's protests have led to many companies banning fur, including H&M, GAP, and designer brands.

PETA uses creative ways to get its message across. A activist, dressed as an animal, targets London Fashion Week, to protest the use of animal fur.

Protecting the World's Animals

World Animal Protection (WAP) is an animal welfare organization that began over 55 years ago. Today, it has 14 offices around the world. Their focus is stopping animal cruelty in all situations. Ending factory farming is a major part of their work. WAP also works to keep wild animals in their natural habitats, and their campaigns help to stop animal trafficking.

Chapter 3

It Starts with You

Animals are suffering around the world, and you want to help. Where do you start? Even small changes to your lifestyle can make a big difference.

You can be an animal rights champion without even leaving home. This means talking to your family and friends about the issues. Spreading awareness is an important way to change things for the better. Many people do not think about the way animals are kept in factory farms, for example. Have a family movie night and talk about animal sentience. Watch something like *My Octopus Teacher*, which shows how amazing these creatures are and why we should protect them.

Consumer Power

Set an example for the people that you know by shopping carefully. Look at the labels on the products that you buy. Support cruelty-free brands. Many countries have banned the making and selling of cosmetics tested on animals. Canada, all countries in the European Union, India, and Australia are some of them.

Vegan shoes are made without using animal products. Instead, they are made with plant-based materials such as cotton or synthetic products.

Animal shelters take in unwanted or stray animals. They often need support, from fundraising to helping at a rehoming center.

Watch What You Wear

Also, think about what you wear. Look for vegan leather or fabric shoes. Many animal rights activists also avoid wearing wool or silk.

Volunteer

See what animal charities and shelters are close by. Your local Humane Society is one place to check out. If you are under 16, you may need a parent or guardian to volunteer with you or sign an approval form. Shelters need people to care for the animals but also to play with them and keep them company. If your family agrees, think about adopting a rescue animal or fostering one until a permanent home can be found.

Going Vegan

A vegan diet contains no meat or dairy. Vegans also avoid eating honey, made by bees, and food that contains gelatin. This is a substance made from the bones or skin of pigs and cows. Marshmallows, jellied desserts, and some candy contain gelatin. Some chocolate and bread contain milk or eggs. Always check for vegan labels and look at the nutrition panel. Avoid products with too much salt or sugar.

A Healthy Choice

If you still eat meat or dairy, consider switching to a vegan, or plant-based, diet part-time. Start by eating less meat and dairy and encouraging your family to do the same. Studies have proven that eating too much meat, especially red meat such as beef, is harmful to our health. Have at least one meat-free day a week and more, if possible. Look up recipes and experiment. Swap a beef burger for a bean burger, for example.

Tennis champion Venus Williams is one of a number of professional athletes who have taken up a vegan diet.

Many food products have a logo to show that they are suitable for vegans. You can also check the list of ingredients to be certain.

More than Vegetables

Vegans eat a lot of vegetables, but a healthy vegan diet includes many other foods. It is important to eat a balanced diet with enough nutrients, such as protein. Vegans do not get their protein from meat, fish, or dairy. They replace these animal foods with plant-based proteins such as nut milks, vegan cheeses, beans, nuts, and lentils. If you like the taste of meat and fish, look for plant-based versions.

Chapter 4

Stand Together

When people come together for a cause, they make those in power take notice. Direct action, from speeches and petitions to marches and protests, can bring about change.

Only a few extreme groups, such as Animal Liberation Front (ALF), have destroyed property and committed other crimes. Most animal rights activism is peaceful and non-violent. This activism is the most successful.

The Humane League

In 2005, a small group of people in Philadelphia started an organization that became The Humane League. Their focus has been the mistreatment of animals raised for food, especially chickens. Small campaigns started at restaurants, asking them to stop serving factory farmed chicken. As The Humane League grew, it spread across the world and petitioned large food companies to put in new animal protection policies.

Campaigns can focus on one issue, like this protest against animal testing, or they can tackle more general subjects, such as animal welfare.

Speak Up

Direct Action Everywhere (DxE)

Priya Sawhney is a co-founder of Direct Action Everywhere (DxE). The group started in California and its campaigns led to the state banning fur. DxE has also rescued many animals from laboratories and animal farms. It has brought together thousands of people across the world. DxE is non-violent but it does disrupt events to spread its animal rights message.

In 2019, Priya Sawhney was arrested after interrupting a speech by Amazon founder and billionaire, Jeff Bezos. She asked him how he was going to use his wealth to stop the abuse of animals on California farms. DxE's goal is to enact an Animal Bill of Rights called Rose's Law. It is named for a hen that was rescued from a chicken farm.

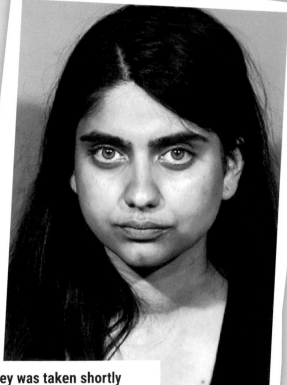

This picture of Priya Sawhney was taken shortly after her arrest for disrupting a speech by Amazon founder, Jeff Bezos. Priya uses direct action to help put animal rights under the spotlight.

Genesis Butler launched Youth Climate Save in 2020. This youth-led organization points out how animal agriculture damages the environment.

Speak Up

Young Animal Activists

Genesis Butler was only six years old when she became a vegan. She was just 10 years old when she gave a TEDx talk about the ways animal agriculture are bad for the planet. She has worked with many organizations, including Mercy for Animals and Farm Sanctuary. She started Genesis for Animals to help animal sanctuaries and rescue centers.

Other young animal rights activists are also making their mark. Carter and Olivia Ries are a brother and sister team that started One More Generation, a group to protect endangered animals. Thomas Ponce runs Lobby for Animals, a group that helps animal rights activists lobby government to change laws. Lou Wegner was a teen actor in California when he started Kids Against Animal Cruelty. He created the online group to help animals in shelters to be adopted.

Youth Activism

Youth-led activism is helping to challenge laws as well as company and government policies. Young actors and musicians use their influence to help to energize the animal rights movement. Many have worked with PETA, including Zendaya, Ariana Grande, Bella Ramsey, and Halle Bailey.

In 2002, peta2 was launched to involve younger people in animal rights activism. The organization is involved at a grassroots level, helping young members with projects they care most about. It offers advice on writing to lawmakers, organizing a petition, and how to support ongoing campaigns. Students Opposing Speciesism (SOS) is part of peta2 and is made up of animal activists aged 13 to 24. It campaigns for many animal rights causes and hopes to spread the message that "animals are not ours to use."

American singer songwriter Billie Eilish is a vegan and advocate of animal rights. She was named PETA's person of the year in 2021.

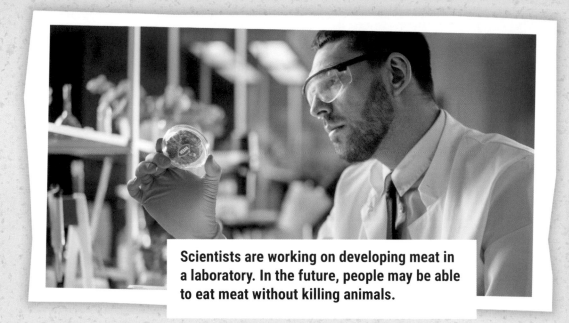

Scientists are working on developing meat in a laboratory. In the future, people may be able to eat meat without killing animals.

Changing the Future

The animal rights movement hopes for a future in which all animals are free and protected. Changing the way people think about animals is part of the fight. This comes through education and action.

The Food Industry

More people than ever are vegans, though the number is still just one to two percent of the world's population. Most people still eat meat and fish, especially in the United States, Canada, China, Australia, Argentina, and many European countries. Making change means finding more ways to spread awareness of things such as factory farming. It means giving people other options, such as plant-based meat or meat grown in a lab.

Factory Farming Awareness Coalition (FFAC) and Leaders for Ethics, Animals, and the Planet (LEAP) are two American organizations that are focused on education. The groups run programs in and out of schools. The programs teach students about the issues of the animal food industry and how they help to develop a food industry that does not include animals.

Speak Up

Root & Shoots

Jane Goodall's Roots & Shoots programs
are aimed at getting young people
involved with protecting Earth, including its animals
and their habitats. The program started over 30 years
ago and now operates in over 65 countries around the
world. It teaches young activists how to develop
projects in their own communities and become
involved in larger campaigns.

Jane Goodall (center) has been an advocate for
animal rights for over 60 years. She founded Roots
& Shoots in 1991. There are now more than 10,000
Roots & Shoots groups around the world.

Chapter 5

Your Activist Toolkit

The world's animals need your help! There are many ways to get involved in the fight for animal justice. Join the millions of young people already working to force positive changes.

You can begin by finding out what animal rights groups, such as a Roots & Shoots chapter, exist in your community. If there is nothing nearby, you can join a group online, but make sure your parent or guardian approves. Also, consider starting your own group with your friends and people at school.

Setting Goals

Animal rights activists fight for rights in different areas. Some focus on animal cruelty in entertainment or factory farming. Others are trying to stop animal trafficking. Think about the issue that you care about the most and focus on that.

Do you want to campaign on general issues or focus on a particular subject? Either way, peta2 has information about how to organize a protest.

The internet is a powerful tool for activists. Use it to research information, find out about campaigns, and to contact other activists.

Educate Yourself

To be an effective animal rights activist, you need to know the facts. Sign up for newsletters from established organizations, such as peta2. Enroll in free online courses for young people on animal rights issues and activism and read as much as you can. Do your research about laws and policies, including local ones.

Gather Resources

What resources do you have and what do you need? People can be a great resource. They can provide information, introduce you to others who can help, and help with ideas. Maybe you know someone who works at your local animal shelter, for example. Also, think about how much time you have and what talents you can offer. Maybe you are a good organizer or perhaps you can teach people how to make vegan food.

Taking Action

Now you have done your research and identified goals, you are ready to act. You can do this in many different ways, from starting your own club to making posters and going on marches.

Start at School

Join or start an animal rights club or a vegan food club at your school. Find out if you can get help from an animal welfare or rights organization. Write a club newsletter to keep people up to date on the latest animal rights news. The club can also fundraise for a particular cause or organization with a movie night or a vegan bake sale. Have an art show where people can submit and donate works of art to sell. Make and sell t-shirts.

Talk to your teacher about holding a vegan food day where people can bring different vegan dishes to share. Make posters about why veganism is healthy for people and the planet. Suggest that the class does a project on animal rights. Split into groups and each can present information on different issues.

Does your school cafeteria offer vegan options? If not, why not start a petition to encourage your school to include vegan choices for lunch.

Collecting names on a petition is a great way to gain support for your campaign. Make sure your demands are clear and you are addressing the petition to the right decision makers.

Social Media

Most official organizations, such as peta2, have social media accounts that you can follow. Always check with a parent or guardian before engaging online. You can make an account for your club to create or repost messages about animal rights. This is way to spread awareness to a large group of people. Make sure you are sending out accurate information and credit your sources.

Take Care of Yourself

Be aware that being an animal rights activist can be difficult. What you see, hear, and read about will be very upsetting. Sometimes it will be hard to stay positive. Make sure you talk to people about how you are feeling and always take a break when you need one.

Timeline

1635 First known animal protection legislation passes, in Ireland, includes a ban on pulling wool off living sheep

1822 British Parliament passes "Act to Prevent the Cruel and Improper Treatment of Cattle"

1824 Royal Society for the Prevention of Cruelty to Animals founded in England

1850 France passes law against the public mistreatment of animals

1866 American Society for the Prevention of Cruelty to Animals founded

1944 Donald Watson founds the Vegan Society in Britain

1954 Humane Society of the United States founded

1964 Ruth Harrison publishes *Animal Machines*

1966 Animal Welfare Act passes in the US

1970 Richard Ryder coins the term "speciesism"

1973 Endangered Species Act passes in the US

1975 Peter Singer publishes *Animal Liberation: A New Ethics for Our Treatment of Animals*

United Nations passes Convention of International Trade in Endangered Species (CITES)

1976 Animal Liberation Front (ALF) founded

1977 Jane Goodall Institute established

1979 Animal Legal Defense Fund founded

1980 People for the Ethical Treatment of Animals (PETA) founded in the United States

1981	The Farm Animal Reform Movement begins
1983	October 2 becomes World Day for Farmed Animals to protest the treatment of farm animals
1985	First Great American MeatOut, an annual day to raise awareness of veganism and cruelty to farmed animals
1986	First Fur Free Friday protest
1989	Avon stops testing its products on animals
1993	General Motors car company in the US stops using live animals in crash tests
1997	European Union Protocol on Animal Protection recognizes animals as sentient beings
1998	United Kingdom bans animal testing for cosmetic products
2006	UK Animal Welfare Act enacted, saying humans have a duty of care of animals
2009	The European Union bans cosmetic ingredients testing and bans the sale or import of seal products
2014	India becomes the first Asian country to ban cosmetic testing on animals
2015	Ringling Brothers, Barnum & Bailey Circus announce phasing out elephants from shows
2016	SeaWorld ends its orca shows and breeding program
2019	Preventing Animal and Cruelty and Torture Act (United States)
	California bans the sale and production of new fur products
2022	Animal Welfare (Sentience) Act, UK, recognizes animal sentience
2023	Canada bans testing cosmetic products on animals

Glossary

activist someone who tries to bring about social change

campaigns works in an organized way toward a specific goal

captivity kept somewhere and not allowed to leave

climate change the change in Earth's climate over a long period of time

ecosystems areas of living and non-living things existing and interacting with together

endangered in danger of becoming extinct, or disappearing

ethical describes behavior that is good and right

factory farming method of farming to produce meat cheaply and quickly

fundraise raising money for a cause

grassroots organized action at a local, community level

greenhouse gases gases such as carbon dioxide, methane, and nitrous oxide that trap heat in the atmosphere

habitat Natural home of an animal or plant

inclusive open to everyone

Indigenous Native to a specific place

lobby engage government officials to change laws or policies for a specific cause

nutrients substances in food that the body needs to stay healthy

petition document signed by a large group of people to make a request for action

political action working with or within government to enact change

sanctuaries safe places for wildlife to live

sentient able to feel and experience emotions

trafficking illegal capture, transportation, and trade

treaty formal agreements between or among nations

vegan not eating or using any animal products

vegetarian not eating meat or fish; may eat eggs and dairy products, such as cheese

welfare relating to health and well-being

Further Information

Books

Harman, Alice. *Animal Cruelty: A Young Activist's Guide.* Franklin Watts, 2020

Kelaher, Catherine. *Saving Animals: A Future Activist's Guide.* Ashland Creek Press, 2021.

Loh-Hagen, Virginia. *Animal Rights.* Cherry Tree, 2021

Newbery, Linda. *This Book is Cruelty Free.* Pavillion, 2021

Websites

www.bosh.tv
A site full of delicious vegan recipes.

www.peta.org/teachkind/ humane-classroom/animal- rights-club/
PETA explains how to start an animal rights club at school.

www.peta2.com
PETA website for young animal rights activists with information and tips about how to get involved.

rootsandshoots.global
Jane Goodall's youth-centered program has local chapters all over the world.

Index